Sorting and Sets

Jackie Walter

Notes for practitioners and parents

This series takes a fun, first look at maths in the environment around us.

Sorting and Sets encourages children to look for sets around them.

Challenge children to sort objects into sets using whatever criteria they choose, for example colour, size, pattern.
You could also start exploring how to record sets and discuss how this can be useful. Count how many objects
are in the different sets and think about ways to show this easily, using tally charts
and pictograms such as those shown on pages 20 and 21.
On a nature walk, collect different objects, for example cones and leaves.
Sort the objects into sets and record the results. Use a book or the Internet to identify the different objects.

Franklin Watts
First published in Great Britain in 2016 by The Watts Publishing Group

Copyright © The Watts Publishing Group 2016

All rights reserved.

Credits
Series Editor: Jackie Hamley
Series Designer: Katie Bennett, Kreative Kupboard
Picture researcher: Diana Morris
Consultant: Kelvin Simms
Photo credits:
Stefan Petru Andronache/Shutterstock: 20cl, 21c, 24tlc, 24brc.
cynoclub/Shutterstock: 22tl, 22bl, 23tr, 23br.
Fabiok/Shutterstock: 22tr.
Paisan Homhuan/Shutterstock: 19cr, 19br.
Jenn Huls/Shutterstock: front cover, 1, 5, 24bc.
In Green/Shutterstock: 3bl, 7 c, 24tc.
Eric Isselee/Shutterstock: 3tl, 20tl, 21t, 23tl, 24tla, 24bra.
Rosa Jay/Shutterstock: 22br.
kilukilu/Shutterstock: 19tl.
Lucie Lang/Shutterstock: 19bl.
mexrix/Shutterstock: 7cl, 24tcl.
oknoart/Shutterstock: 3br, 9.
Fesus Robert/Shutterstock: 20tlb, 21tb, 24tl, 24br.
Elena Schweitzer/Shutterstock: 2tr, 2b, 17.
s74/Shutterstock: 11.
Sandra van der Steen/Shutterstock: 3tr, 19tr.

Kuttelvaserova Stuchelova/Shutterstock: 20bl, 21b; 24tlb, 24brb.
Susii/Shutterstock: 2tl, 7tr, 24tcr.
Praiwun Thungsam/Shutterstock: 19c.
Vlad61/Shutterstock: 13, 24bl.
Pan Xunbin/Shutterstock: 23bl, 23cr.
Tewam Yangmee/Shutterstock: 15, 24tr.

Disclaimer.

Every attempt has been made to clear copyright.
Should there be any inadvertent omission please apply to the publisher
for rectification.

Dewey number 511.3'2
ISBN 978 1 4451 4925 7

Printed in China

Franklin Watts
An imprint of Hachette Children's Group, Part of The Watts Publishing
Group
Carmelite House, 50 Victoria Embankment, London EC4Y 0DZ
An Hachette UK Company
www.hachette.co.uk   www.franklinwatts.co.uk

Contents

Sorting

We can put things into different groups by looking at what colour, shape or size they are.

We can also group things by looking at what they are used for or what they do.

Putting things into groups is called sorting.

Making a Set

When we group or sort things, we make them into a set. A set is a group of things that are the same in some way.

What is the same in this set of things?

Same or Different?

When we sort objects into a set, we look for things about the objects that are the same or things that are different.

What is the same about these robots?

What is different?

Useful Sets

Sorting things into sets can help us.
At the supermarket, all the food is sorted into
sets so that we can find things easily.
The food is sorted by what kind of food it is.

Can you think what sets this food is sorted into?

Sorting by Size

We can sort things by their size.
These fish could be sorted into two sets -
big and little fish.

Can you think of other things it would be
useful to sort by size?

Sorting by Shape

We can also sort things by shape.
Look at these chocolates.

How many shapes can you see?

How else could you sort these chocolates into sets?

Large and Small Sets

Large sets can often be sorted into smaller sets.
This is a set of musical instruments.
It could be sorted into smaller sets, such as
instruments we shake, instruments we blow
or instruments we hit.

More than One Set

Sometimes, things can belong to more than one set.
All the dinosaur toys in the blue circle are green.
All the dinosaurs in the red circle have spikes.
The dinosaur in both circles is green and has spikes.

Recording a Set

There are different ways to record sets. Recording sets can help us to show lots of information easily. In these two different charts, we can quickly show who in the class likes which pet best.

Pet	Number of Likes
	IIII II
	IIII
	III
	II

This chart is called a tally chart.

Which pet is the favourite? How many children like cats best?
How many children are in the class?

Pet	Number of Likes

This chart is called a pictogram.

What Sorting Tells Us

Sorting things into sets tells us more about them. Sorting these animals into sets helps us to recognise what is different and what is the same about them – whether they have feathers, hair or scales, whether they live on land or under water.

Sorting helps to tell us about our world.

Word Bank

pictogram

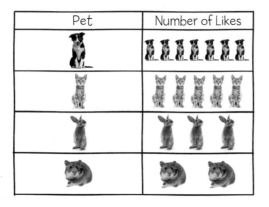

set

shape

size

sorting

tally chart

Pet	Number of Likes
🐕	卌 II
🐈	卌
🐇	III
🐹	II

24